CW00890984

Morning, Noon & Night

PATTERNS FOR DAILY DEVOTION

Michael Forster

Kevin
Mayhew

First published in 1993 by
KEVIN MAYHEW LTD
Rattlesden
Bury St Edmunds
Suffolk IP30 0SZ

© 1993 Kevin Mayhew Ltd

All rights reserved.
No part of this publication
may be reproduced, stored in a retrieval system,
or transmitted, in any form or by any means,
electronic, mechanical, photocopying, recording
or otherwise, without the prior written permission
of the publisher.

Front cover: *Gift House Brethren*
by William Banks Fortescue (fl. 1880-1901).
Reproduced by courtesy of Fine Art
Photographic Library, London

ISBN   0 86209 445 3

Cover design by Graham Johnstone
Typesetting and Page Creation by Anne Haskell
Printed and bound in Great Britain.

CONTENTS

Foreword

Prayer is an entering into the mind of God: much more than merely 'talking to God', and certainly more than presenting a kind of shopping list. This book is intended to encourage an opening up to God who speaks through scripture, but also through people and events, and through our own deepening self-knowledge.

It is not always a comfortable experience, but it should be positive, if our gospel is one of grace.

Confession, for example, should be an un-burdening of ourselves onto God, not a stirring-up of useless and destructive guilt. Of course it must be honest, and will often be painful, but in the end we rest on the redemptive power of a love which we cannot comprehend and do not need to deserve.

Commitment, similarly, is not the dutiful shouldering of a burden, but the joyful acceptance of God's invitation to be partners in creation.

It is in that kind of spirit that this book is offered. It should not, therefore, be simply read through, but given time in honest openness before God. Hopefully it will also stimulate further exploration of scripture, of various prayer traditions, and of the inner self.

Following the daily structure, there is a further section of additional prayers, meditations and readings. These may be used at any time during the day, as appropriate, or can be used to supplement or replace material in the morning or evening.

MICHAEL FORSTER

Daily Patterns for Prayer

Sunday Morning

ANTICIPATING

Today is a day of rest; a day for worship, for recreation, for friendship; a chance to live differently, to relate to others, simply to be. Or perhaps it must be a work-day – for the well-being of others. Aim to be sensitive to those for whom the other days have been full of activity, and who need this time out. And if not today, when will you take your rest?

THANKSGIVING

Thank you, God, for life:
    resurrection life,
    triumphing over fear,
    over pressure,
    over futility.
Thank you for rhythm
    of times and seasons,
    of work and leisure,
    of ambition and contentment.
Thank you, God,
    for life.

READING

Mary stood outside the tomb crying. She turned around and saw Jesus standing there, but she did not realize that it was Jesus. 'Woman,' he said, 'why are you crying? Who is it you are looking for?' Thinking he was the gardener, she said, 'Sir, if you have carried him away, tell me

where you have put him, and I will get him.'
Jesus said to her, 'Mary.' She turned toward him
and cried out in Aramaic, 'Rabboni!' (which
means Teacher). Jesus said, 'Do not hold on to
me, for I have not yet returned to the Father.
Go instead to my brothers and tell them, "I am
returning to my Father and your Father, to my
God and your God."'   John 20:11,14-17

MEDITATING

*How do we celebrate new life? Will this day be
different from the past six? What are the qualities
which mark out resurrection life?*

INTERCEDING

God of all creation,
I pray for all who live under pressure,
    whether from work or family,
    whether from religion or other commitments,
    and especially the pressure of poverty.
Give them time to relax,
    time to look and listen,
    time to love and be loved.

COMMITTING

God, let this be your day:
    truly glorifying to you,
    and a burden to no-one.

SUNDAY EVENING

RECOLLECTING
Call to mind encounters of the day, with family, friends, passers-by and others.

THANKSGIVING
Thank you, loving God
for all that has been good today:
for friends and family . . .
for leisure,
for the fellowship of the church,
and especially . . .

UNBURDENING
O God, today has been less than perfect.
But it is gone.
If there is damage I can repair,
give me grace to do so at the right time
Now let me rest,
assured that you love me
as I am.

READING
But now, this is what the Lord says – he who created you, O Jacob, he who formed you, O Israel: 'Fear not, for I have redeemed you; I have summoned you by name; you are mine. When you pass through the waters, I will be with you; and when you pass through the rivers, they will not sweep over you. When you walk through the fire, you will not be burned;

the flames will not set you ablaze. For I am the Lord, your God, the Holy One of Israel, your Saviour; I give Egypt for your ransom, Cush and Seba in your stead. Since you are precious and honoured in my sight, and because I love you, I will give men in exchange for you, and people in exchange for your life. Do not be afraid, for I am with you; I will bring your children from the east and gather you from the west. Isaiah 43:1-5

MEDITATING

Unconditional love for undeserving people. Why should we not rest with such a promise!

ENTRUSTING

Into your hands, O God,
> I entrust all that is precious to me:
my friends and family,
> my hopes, my dreams, and my fears,
into your hands.

MONDAY MORNING

ANTICIPATING

What does the week ahead hold? Does it have space planned into it? Is today fresh, or is there unfinished business from last week to attend to? Is the prospect, whether of work or the lack of it, pleasing or not?

THANKSGIVING

Thank you, holy God,
    for the rhythm of life.
Thank you for hope.
However the week looks,
    promising or unpromising
I will find you within it.

READING

The Lord abhors dishonest scales, but accurate weights are his delight. When pride comes, then comes disgrace, but with humility comes wisdom. The integrity of the upright guides them, but the unfaithful are destroyed by their duplicity. Wealth is worthless in the day of wrath, but righteousness delivers from death. The righteousness of the blameless makes a straight way for them, but the wicked are brought down by their own wickedness. The righteousness of the upright delivers them, but the unfaithful are trapped by evil desires. When a wicked man dies, his hope perishes; all he expected from his power comes to nothing.
Proverbs 11:1-7

MEDITATING
Any kind of activity will bring choices; some easy, some not. What might be the opportunities and temptations of the day?

INTERCEDING
For some, this day will be full,
        for others, empty.
For some, the rhythm is hectic,
        for others there is no rhythm.
Each says to other,
        'I'd like your problems!'
Make me sensitive,
        understanding of all people.
and may all life find meaning,
        in you.

COMMITTING
Eternal God,
        no less than yesterday,
        although differently,
        this is your day.
Whatever it holds,
        let it be the kind of day
        I shall not be afraid
        to offer to you at its end.

Monday Evening

RECOLLECTING
Did what happened today meet your expectations?
What was different? What were the special joys, the
particular hurts?

THANKSGIVING
God I thank you:
for the 'highs'
    and the 'lows',
for your presence,
    in all things,
    and in all people,
for shared happiness,
    for grace and patience,
for the hope of good
    born out of failure.

UNBURDENING
Today has not been perfect.
I have said and done
    things, which I regret.
I cannot change them,
    at this moment.
Take them from me, tonight,
    and tomorrow
    let me make amends.
If anything is irreparable,
    in human terms,
help me to trust your love
    for redemption.

READING

Lord, you have assigned me my portion and my cup; you have made my lot secure. The boundary lines have fallen for me in pleasant places; surely I have a delightful inheritance. I will praise the Lord, who counsels me; even at night my heart instructs me. I have set the Lord always before me. Because he is at my right hand, I will not be shaken. Therefore my heart is glad and my tongue rejoices; my body also will rest secure, because you will not abandon me to the grave, nor will you let your Holy One see decay. You have made known to me the path of life; you will fill me with joy in your presence, with eternal pleasures at your right hand.   Psalm 16:5-11

MEDITATING

In the psalmist's times, the night was perilous indeed. Despite all that the media tell us, most of us are in remarkably little danger, by comparison. Whatever the appearances, this is still God's world.

ENTRUSTING

Lord, I believe in you.
Help what unbelief I have.

Tuesday Morning

ANTICIPATING

Every day is full of possibilities. What might they be? How far do they depend on your own attitude or approach?

THANKSGIVING

Thank you, God,
for opportunity.
Here is a new day,
untouched by my hand,
but held in yours.
I need you,
And you have chosen to need me.
Together, we can bring to fruition
some of life's endless possibilities.
Thank you, God.

READING

As Pharaoh approached, the Israelites looked up, and there were the Egyptians, marching after them. They were terrified and cried out to the Lord. They said to Moses, 'Was it because there were no graves in Egypt that you brought us to the desert to die? What have you done to us by bringing us out of Egypt? Didn't we say to you in Egypt, "Leave us alone; let us serve the Egyptians"? It would have been better for us to serve the Egyptians than to die in the desert!' Moses answered the people, 'Do not be afraid. Stand firm and you will see the deliverance the

Lord will bring you today. The Egyptians you see today you will never see again. The Lord will fight for you; you need only to be still.' Then the Lord said to Moses, 'Why are you crying out to me? Tell the Israelites to move on.'   Exodus 14:10-15

MEDITATING

Prayer is a wonderful thing. But there comes a time to act. We need faith to go into the unknown, trusting God to be there for us.

INTERCEDING

Hear my prayer, O God,
    for all who fear life,
       through guilt or low self-esteem,
for all who are enslaved
    by 'the devil they know',
and dare not take the risk
    of journeying with you.
Have mercy, O God,
    for we are many.

COMMITTING

Liberating God,
    I will go with you.
I will trust you,
    whatever comes,
not shirking the responsibilities,
    or fearing the risks.

Tuesday Evening

RECOLLECTING

What were the unexpected events of the day? Were there any discoveries of strength or weakness?

THANKSGIVING

Thank you, faithful God,
> for being you.
You choose to be a loving God,
> a forgiving God,
> an ever-present help.
Thank you, faithful God,
> for being you.

UNBURDENING

God, forgive me,
> whenever I have doubted you;
whenever I have 'done it my way',
> while knowing yours was different.
For my little trust in you,
> for my excessive trust in me,
God, forgive me,
> and let me sleep.

READING

I am convinced that neither death nor life, neither angels nor demons, neither the present nor the future, nor any powers, neither height nor depth, nor anything else in all creation, will be able to separate us from the love of God that is in Christ Jesus our Lord.   Romans 8:38-39

MEDITATING
Nothing in creation; nothing in us, or in the world around us! Rest in the love of God.

ENTRUSTING
Holy God, I give the past day to you:
    its successes and its failures,
    its unfinished business,
    its remaining anxieties.
Take them,
    do with them as you will,
    and let me rest.

Wednesday Morning

ANTICIPATING

Many things will happen today: people will be born and will die, will gain and will lose; many will rejoice, and many will be sad. That's how the world is. And God is part of it.

THANKSGIVING

Ever-present God,
    thank you for being here.
Thank you for sharing joys,
    and for enduring pain.
Thank you for making me
    part of the world.
Thank you for keeping me in touch.

READING

With what shall I come before the Lord and bow down before the exalted God? Shall I come before him with burnt offerings, with calves a year old? Will the Lord be pleased with thousands of rams, with ten thousand rivers of oil? Shall I offer my firstborn for my transgression, the fruit of my body for the sin of my soul? He has showed you, O man, what is good. And what does the Lord require of you? To act justly and to love mercy and to walk humbly with your God.   Micah 6:6-8

MEDITATING

What does that mean, practically, in today's particular situation? Think about the people you are likely to meet, the situations you might encounter, the dilemmas you may have to face. What opportunities might today bring to act justly, and to love mercy?

INTERCEDING

I pray for the world:
>for the poor and the homeless,
>the oppressed and the exploited.

Give me grace to respond,
>in a positive way,
>to their needs.

COMMITTING

Today I will live:
>truly live;

as part of God's creation,
>in co-operation with others,
>in solidarity with the poor,
>at one with God.

Anything else would be death.

Today I will live:
>truly live.

WEDNESDAY EVENING

RECOLLECTING
What was in the news today? How was Christ visible in it: living, crucified and risen in his people?

THANKSGIVING
Thank you, God,
for being 'Christlike'.
Thank you for showing yourself
in life,
in death,
in celebration,
in sorrow,
in hope.
Thank you for calling me to share
in all of that.

UNBURDENING
O Christ, forgive:
where you have been ignored,
obscured,
rejected
among your people,
because of me.
Tell me that it mattered,
tell me that it hurt,
but most of all,
tell me of hope.
Tomorrow is another day.

READING

When they had finished eating, Jesus said to
Simon Peter, 'Simon son of John, do you truly
love me more than these?' 'Yes, Lord,' he said,
'you know that I love you.' Jesus said, 'Feed my
lambs.' Again Jesus said, 'Simon son of John, do
you truly love me?' He answered, 'Yes, Lord,
you know that I love you.' Jesus said, 'Take care
of my sheep.' The third time he said to him,
'Simon son of John, do you love me?' Peter was
hurt because Jesus asked him the third time,
'Do you love me?' He said, 'Lord, you know all
things; you know that I love you.' Jesus said,
'Feed my sheep.'   John 21:15-17

MEDITATING

*Three denials, three opportunities for repentance,
three calls to service. Nothing is beyond forgiveness,
and for every failure there is a new opportunity. Rest
on that promise.*

ENTRUSTING

To you, O risen Christ,
I entrust all my failings.
Use them to create life.

Thursday Morning

Anticipating

The day is seldom if ever trouble-free. If anything worthwhile is going to happen, there must always be at least the risk of pain. In business, family life, education, wherever people try to create something good, there is a risk. That will be so today. The question is, 'Is it worth it?' The answer, in God's providence, is 'Yes.'

Thanksgiving

Thank you, God,
>   for incarnation:
For taking the risk
>   of being human,
>   of making friends,
>   of offering love,
>   of living in hope.
Thank you for being here,
>   for calling me to do that, too.
Thank you, God,
>   for incarnation.

Reading

For a long time I have kept silent, I have been quiet and held myself back. But now, like a woman in childbirth, I cry out, I gasp and pant. I will lay waste the mountains and hills and dry up all their vegetation; I will turn rivers into islands and dry up the pools. I will lead the blind by ways they have not known, along unfamiliar paths I will guide them; I will turn the darkness into light before them and make the rough places smooth. These are the things I will do; I will not forsake them.   Isaiah 42:14-16

MEDITATING

The gospel speaks of troubles in the world as 'birth-pains'. Can we face whatever the day holds for us with that kind of trust? And how long are we prepared labour with God for the 'child' to be born?

INTERCEDING

O God, I pray in hope,
for all who will feel pain today:
> for parents and children,
> for the sick and the poor,
> for the exploited.
I pray for all who seek to make hope real.
I pray in hope,
> to be a sign of hope.

COMMITTING

I don't know what will happen today,
> but I will try to use it for good,
and if I can't do that,
> I'll trust you.
For as long as it takes.

Thursday Evening

RECOLLECTING

How does the day look now? Are you glad it's over, or glad it happened, or perhaps something of both? What were the struggles of the day, and what the rewards?

THANKSGIVING

Thank you, holy God.
A lot has happened today,
 to me and to others.
Thank you for joy,
 and thank you for hope.
It may be hard at times to see it,
 but thank you that it is there.
Thank you that *you* are there.

UNBURDENING

It isn't easy to be faithful,
 or to be hopeful.
It isn't easy to trust
  in someone you can't see,
  in the midst of a load of trouble
  that you can see.
I feel guilty about it.
  I want to make amends.
  But I can't.
Take the guilt and the fear, O God,
  let me sleep well,

and wake me in the morning
> to new life, and new hope.

READING

Praise the Lord, O my soul; all my inmost
being, praise his holy name. Praise the Lord, O
my soul, and forget not all his benefits – who
forgives all your sins and heals all your diseases,
who redeems your life from the pit and crowns
you with love and compassion, who satisfies
your desires with good things so that your youth
is renewed like the eagle's.   Psalm 103:1-5

MEDITATING

*Work addicts resent time spent sleeping, regarding it
as 'lost' time. But God redeems what is lost, using it
to bring about renewal of life.*

ENTRUSTING

I rest in hope.
You will complete
> what the day leaves unfinished.

You will heal
> what the day has broken.

I rest in hope.

Friday Morning

What is in the diary for today? What kind of people are involved? Might there be friction, misunderstanding, even pain?

THANKSGIVING
Thank you, God,
    for the people around me:
for those who are closest
    and best loved;
for those who are distant,
    or difficult to love.
Thank you for the opportunities
    each presents,
of loving unconditionally,
    of living creatively.
Thank you, God,
    for the people around me.

READING
Near the cross of Jesus stood his mother, his mother's sister, Mary the wife of Clopas, and Mary Magdalene. When Jesus saw his mother there, and the disciple whom he loved standing nearby, he said to his mother, 'Dear woman, here is your son,' and to the disciple, 'Here is your mother.' From that time on, this disciple took her into his home.   John 19:25-27

MEDITATING

Where is the crucified Christ found among his people now? Who are the mothers and sons for whom he calls us to care? Who are they locally, and further afield? And can you, like the beloved disciple, do something practical today?

INTERCEDING

Suffering God,
 the news is full of you;
 the papers are full of you.
You call us to recognise you,
 to recognise each other;
 you call us to care.
O God, I pray:
 food for the hungry,
 homes for the homeless,
 comfort for the sorrowing,
 dignity for the dying,
and a part for me to play, in all that.

COMMITTING

Today I will do a little
 more than before.
I can't stop the world's pain,
 I can't solve its problems
But I will do something.
 However little.

Friday Evening

RECOLLECTING
What were the signs of hope, today? How or in whom,
was God visibly present even in the bad things?

THANKSGIVING
Thank you, God,
    for being here.
Not always easy to look at,
    sometimes challenging and disturbing,
calling me to care
    for mothers and sons,
    brothers and sisters;
trusting me
    with precious people.
Thank you, God,
    for being here.

UNBURDENING
There's so much left to do:
    so much suffering,
    so much injustice,
    so much despair;
and I have done so little.
    And even that wasn't flawless.
Take the incompleteness of today,
    of my work for you,
    of myself,
and point me towards another day,
    a different day,

a better day.
And in that hope
let me rest.

READING

Later, knowing that all was now completed, and
so that the Scripture would be fulfilled, Jesus
said, 'I am thirsty.' A jar of wine vinegar was
there, so they soaked a sponge in it, put the
sponge on a stalk of the hyssop plant, and lifted
it to Jesus' lips. When he had received the
drink, Jesus said, 'It is finished.' With that, he
bowed his head and gave up his spirit.
John 19:28-30

MEDITATING

*The work of redemption is sealed. Good has
withstood the worst assault of evil. Think of Martin
Luther King, of Mother Teresa, of Oscar Romero,
refusing to compromise, making wholehearted
sacrifices, following the way of the cross. There is still
work to do, but clearly the decisive battle has indeed
been won.*

ENTRUSTING

Into your hands, O God,
I commend . . .
everything.

Saturday Morning

ANTICIPATING

*What does the day hold? Work? Leisure? Commit-
ments? Freedom? Perhaps a mixture. Will it be like
all the others, or different?*

THANKSGIVING

Thank you, God,
    for variety;
    the wonderful varied-ness of creation.
No two things you make
    are ever precisely the same.
Today will be different,
    in some way or other.
Not because I make it so,
    but because you do.
Thank you, God,
    for variety.

READING

Therefore do not worry, saying, 'What will we
eat?' or 'What will we drink?' or 'What will we
wear?' For it is the Gentiles who strive for all
these things; and indeed your heavenly Father
knows that you need all these things. But strive
first for the kingdom of God and his
righteousness, and all these things will be given
to you as well.   Matthew 6:31-33

MEDITATING

'The kingdom of God' . . . a relationship with God which expresses itself in all other relationships: with family, friends, community and the whole created order. So many of the world's problems come down to a lack of trust – a failed relationship – somewhere in creation. Dare we trust completely, or do we always hold back a little, just in case?

INTERCEDING

Such a complex world.
> So many people,
> so many interactions,
> so many possibilities for error.

We dare not trust ourselves,
> and we're not ready to trust you.

Creator and Redeemer of all things,
> fill us with your Spirit,
> give us grace to trust you,
> and lead creation from death to life.

COMMITTING

Today I will relax a little more,
> trust a little more.

It won't be easy,
> and there may not be instant results.

That's why I need grace.

Saturday Evening

RECOLLECTING
Not just the day, but the week as well. Where has God been encountered, in people, in events, in sights and sounds?

THANKSGIVING
Thank you, God,
for everything:
    for the beauty of creation,
    for the changing of the weather,
    for the variety of moods and feelings.
Thank you for people,
    many different people,
    of many cultures,
    many traditions,
    many faiths.
Thank you for love,
    for friendship,
    for community,
    for yourself.
Thank you, God,
    for everything.

UNBURDENING
It isn't always easy
    to be faithful,
    to be loving,
    to be human.

I've tried.
Sometimes, I've succeeded,
  but often I've failed.
I know it matters.
I know there will be consequences
  from my failings.
Only one thing I ask:
  let me stand again in your presence,
  assured of your love,
  as I am.
Only then will I know
  what I may become.

READING
But I am not ashamed, for I know the one in whom I have put my trust, and I am sure that he is able to guard until that day what I have entrusted to him.   2 Timothy 1:12

MEDITATING
On whose achievements, whose trustworthiness, does everything ultimately depend?

ENTRUSTING
My God, I entrust myself to you.
  I can do no more.

Prayer During the Day

Prayers, Meditations and Devotional Readings

YOU KNOW ME

O Lord, you have searched me and you know me.
You know when I sit and when I rise;
  you perceive my thoughts from afar.
You discern my going out and my lying down;
  you are familiar with all my ways.
Before a word is on my tongue
  you know it completely, O Lord.

You hem me in – behind and before;
  you have laid your hand upon me.
Such knowledge is too wonderful for me,
  too lofty for me to attain.

Where can I go from your Spirit?
  Where can I flee from your presence?

If I go up to the heavens, you are there;
  if I make my bed in the depths, you are there.
If I rise on the wings of the dawn,
  if I settle on the far side of the sea,
even there your hand will guide me,
  your right hand will hold me fast.

Psalm 139:1-10

PRAYER FOR PEACE

Lead me from death to life,
    from falsehood to truth;
lead me from despair to hope,
    from fear to trust;
lead me from hate to love;
    from war to peace;
let peace fill our hearts,
    our world, our universe.

Peace . . . peace . . . peace.

SAYINGS OF
MOTHER TERESA

Every work of love brings a person face to face
with God.

Simple acts of love and care keep the light of
Christ burning.

Together we can do something beautiful for God.

YOU WANT US TO CHANGE

God – you want us to change;
    you want us to let our lives be loved
     and forgiven;
    you want to heal our hurt.

God – we feel threatened;
    we have found ways to protect ourselves;
    we have our own safety measures
    and most of the time they work.

God – we do not want to change.
    Your love is a risk.
    It makes us vulnerable;
    we have been hurt before;
    we can remember the pain.

God – you want us to be different;
    deep inside, we want that too.
    Help us to hold your hand.

The Iona Community Worship Book

MAKE ME WILLING

When I want to do
   only great things, Lord,
make me willing to do
   small, unnoticed things, too.
When I want to do
   what the world will acclaim,
make me willing to do
   what will lift up your name.

FAITH AND WORKS

Living God, you have taught us that faith without works is dead, so temper our faith with love and hope that we follow Christ and give ourselves freely to people in their need: then the lives we live may honour you for ever. Amen

The Iona Community Worship Book

WE TURN TO YOU, O GOD

O God, we bring you our failure,
    our hunger, our disappointment, our despair,
    our greed, our aloofness, our loneliness.
When we cling to others in desperation
    or turn from them in fear
strengthen us in love.
Teach us, women and men,
    to use our power with care.

We turn to you, O God,
    we renounce evil,
    we claim your love,
    we choose to be made whole.

Women Included, The St. Hilda Community

Jesus said, 'Father, forgive them for they do not know what they are doing.'

Luke 23:34

PRAYER OF
FRANCIS OF ASSISI

Lord, make me an instrument of your peace:
Where there is hatred,
   let me sow love:
where there is injury,
   pardon:
where there is doubt,
   faith:
where there is darkness,
   light:
where there is despair,
   hope:
and where there is sadness,
   joy.

O divine Master,
grant that I may not so much seek
   to be consoled as to console,
   to be understood as to understand,
   to be loved as to love.
For it is in giving
   that we receive,
It is in pardoning
   that we are pardoned,
and in dying
   that we are born to eternal life.

NOT DEATH THROES
BUT BIRTH PANGS

Lord:
help us to see in the groaning of creation
    not death throes by birth pangs;
help us to see in suffering a promise for the future,
    because it is a cry against the inhumanity of
      the present.
Help us to glimpse in protest the dawn of justice,
    in the cross the pathway to resurrection,
    and in suffering the seeds of joy.

Rubem Alves, Brazil based on *Romans 8:18-25*

GOD GRANT ME
SERENITY

God grant me
    serenity to accept the things I cannot change
courage to change the things I can,
    and wisdom to know the difference.

THE GATE OF THE YEAR

I said to the man who stood
    at the gate of the year,
'Give me a light, that I may travel
    safely into the unknown.'
And he replied,
    'Go out into the darkness,
and put your hand
    into the hand of God.
That shall be to you better than light,
    and safer than a known way.'

So I went forth, and
    finding the hand of God,
    trod gladly into the night.
And he led me towards the hills,
    and the breaking of day in the lone East.

Minnie Louise Haskins

Our Father, it is your universe,
    it is your will, let us be at peace;
let the souls of your people be cool;
you are our Father,
remove all evil from our path.

Heart of Prayer: Dinka, Sudan

Your Will Be Done

Teach us, good Lord,
    to serve you as you deserve:
to give,
    and not to count the cost,
to fight,
    and not to heed the wounds,
to toil,
    and not to seek for rest,
to labour,
    and to ask for no reward,
except that of knowing
    that we do your will.

Trust The Past

Trust the past
    to the mercy of God,
the present to his love,
    the future to his providence.

PRAYER OF
RICHARD OF CHICHESTER

Thanks be to you,
    my Lord Jesus Christ,
for all the benefits
    you have given to me;
for all the pains and insults
    you have borne for me.

O most merciful redeemer,
    friend and brother,
may I know you more clearly,
    love you more dearly
and follow you more nearly,
    all my days.

NEVER TOO BUSY TO CARE

Lord, make me so sensitive
    to the needs of those around me
that I never fail to know
    when they're hurting or afraid;
or when they're simply crying out
    for someone's touch
    to ease their loneliness.
Let me love so much
    that my first thought is of others
    and my last thought is of me.

GOD'S PROMISE

'The days are coming,' declares the Lord,
   'when the reaper will be overtaken by the
     ploughman
   and the planter by the one treading grapes.
New wine will drip from the mountains
   and flow from all the hills.
I will bring back my exiled people Israel;
   they will rebuild the ruined cities
   and live in them.
They will plant vineyards
   and drink their wine;
They will make gardens
   and eat their fruit.
I will plant Israel
   in their own land,
never again to be uprooted
   from the land I have given them.'

Amos 9:13-15

CHRIST BE WITH ME

Christ be with me,
Christ within me,
Christ behind me,
Christ before me,
Christ beside me,
Christ to win me,
Christ to comfort
    and restore me,

Christ beneath me,
Christ above me,
Christ in quiet,
Christ in danger,
Christ in hearts
    of all that love me,
Christ in mouth
    of friend and stranger.

ENJOY THE EARTH GENTLY

Enjoy the earth gently.
Enjoy the earth gently,
    for if the earth is spoiled
    it cannot be repaired.
Enjoy the earth gently.

Yoruba Poem, West Africa

TO LIVE IN COMMUNITY

Lord, you placed me in the world to live in
    community.
Thus you taught me to love,
    to share in life,
    to struggle for bread and for justice,
    your truth incarnate in my life.
So be it, Jesus.
Amen

Living the Good News

DO NOT BOAST

Do not boast about tomorrow,
   for you do not know
   what a day may bring forth.

Let another praise you,
   and not your own mouth;
someone else,
   and not your own lips.

Proverbs 27:1-2

GLORY BE TO YOU

Glory be to you,
   Ground of all Being,
   Source of all Strength,
   Giver of all Power.
Amen.

Women Included: The St Hilda Community

MY TIME

'My time', we say.
    How presumptuous!
It's not ours:
    we didn't make it,
    we can't stop it;
    no-one can preserve it.
We can't hold the present moment,
    it slips through our fingers.
We can't freeze it,
    or bottle it,
    to await our pleasure.
We can't even define it:
    'animal, vegetable or mineral'!
Does it exist?
If it does,
    whose is it?

God, teach us to value it,
    to love it,
    to relax in its embrace,
and always to remember
    that it's not ours.

It's yours.

Michael Forster

HAVE MERCY ON US

I lift up my eyes to you,
to you whose throne is in heaven.

As the eyes of slaves
look to the hand of their master,
as the eyes of a maid
look to the hand of her mistress,
so our eyes look to the Lord our God,
till he shows us his mercy.

Have mercy on us, O Lord,
have mercy on us,
for we have endured much contempt.
We have endured much ridicule from the proud,
much contempt from the arrogant.

Psalm 123

BLESS OUR HOME

Bless our home, Father,
that we cherish the bread
   before there is none,
discover each other
   before we leave,
and enjoy each other
   for what we are,
    while we have time.

CREATOR, WHERE SHALL I FIND YOU?

Creator, where shall I find you?
   High and hidden is your place.
And where shall I not find you?
   The earth is full of your glory.

I have sought your nearness,
   with all my heart I sought you,
and going out to meet you,
   I found you coming to meet me.

Judah Halevi

TIME

It's a strange, elusive thing:
    we can share it,
    we can spend it,
    we can give it,
    we can use it,
We can do all kinds of things with it,
    but we can't make it,
    we can't repeat it,
    we can't really save it.

All too often,
    we abuse it,
    we waste it,
    we kill it.
We can't get it back.

Holy God,
    when you redeem all things
    redeem time.

Michael Forster

DELIGHT IN THE
LAW OF THE LORD

Blessed is the man who does not walk
    in the counsel of the wicked
or stand in the way of sinners
or sit in the seat of mockers.

But his delight is in the law of the Lord,
    and on his law he meditates day and night.
He is like a tree planted by streams of water,
    which yields its fruit in season
    and whose leaf does not wither.

Psalm 1:1-3

Let us behave gently
    that we may die peacefully;
that our children may stretch out their hands
    upon us in burial.

Heart of Prayer: Yoruba, Nigeria

KING DAVID'S BLESSING

Yours, O Lord, is the greatness and the power and the glory and the majesty and the splendour, for everything in heaven and earth is yours. Yours, O Lord, is the kingdom; you are exalted as head over all. Wealth and honour come from you; you are the ruler of all things. In your hands are strength and power to exalt and give strength to all. Now, our God, we give you thanks, and praise your glorious name.

1 Chronicles 29:11-13

I urge, then, first of all, that requests, prayers, intercession and thanksgiving be made for everyone – for kings and all those in authority, that we may live peaceful and quiet lives in all godliness and holiness. This is good, and pleases God our Saviour.

1 Timothy 2:1-3

'TWAS I

'Twas I that shed the sacred blood:
    I nailed him to the tree;
I crucified the Christ of God,
    I joined the mockery.

Of all that shouting multitude
    I feel that I am one;
and in that din of voices rude
    I recognise my own.

Around the cross the throng I see,
    mocking the Sufferer's groan;
yet still my voice it seems to be,
    as if I mocked alone.

Horatius Bonar

But you are a chosen people, a royal priesthood, a holy nation, a people belonging to God, that you may declare the praises of him who called you out of darkness into his wonderful light.

1 Peter 2:9

DEEP PEACE

Deep peace of the running wave to you.
Deep peace of the flowing air to you.
Deep peace of the quiet earth to you.
Deep peace of the shining stars to you.
Deep peace of the Son of peace to you.

A GAELIC BLESSING

May the road rise to meet you,
may the wind be always at your back,
may the sun shine warm upon your face,
may the rain fall softly upon your fields,
and may God hold you in the hollow of his hand.

TRUST IN GOD

The Lord is my shepherd,
    I shall not be in want.
He makes me lie down in green pastures,
    he leads me beside quiet waters,
    he restores my soul.
He guides me in paths of righteousness
    for his name's sake.
Even though I walk through the valley
    of the shadow of death,
I will fear no evil,
    for you are with me;
    your rod and your staff, they comfort me.
You prepare a table before me
    in the presence of my enemies.
You anoint my head with oil;
    my cup overflows.
Surely goodness and love will follow me
    all the days of my life,
and I will dwell in the house of the Lord forever.

Psalm 23

WILT THOU FORGIVE

Wilt thou forgive that sin where I begun,
    which was my sin, though it were done before?
Wilt thou forgive that sin through which I run
    and do run still, though still I do deplore?
When thou hast done, thou hast not done,
    for I have more.

wilt thou forgive that sin which I have won
    others to sin, and made my sin their door?
Wilt thou forgive that sin which I did shun
    a year or two, but wallowed in a score?
When thou hast done, thou hast not done,
    for I have more.

I have a sin of fear, that when I've spun
    my last thread, I shall perish on the shore;
but swear by thyself that at my death thy Son
    shall shine as he shines now and heretofore;
and having done that, thou hast done:
    I fear no more.

John Donne

Note the pun on the author's own name, and on "Son"

INDIFFERENCE

When Jesus came to Golgotha they hanged him
    on a tree,
      they drove great nails through hands and feet
      and made a Calvary;
they crowned him with a crown of thorns,
      red were his wounds and deep,
    for those were crude and cruel days,
      and human flesh was cheap.

When Jesus came to Birmingham they simply
    passed him by,
      they never hurt a hair of him,
      they only let him die,
for men had grown more tender and they would
    not give him pain,
      they only just passed down the street,
      and left him in the rain.

Still Jesus cried, 'Forgive them, for they know not
    what they do,'
    and still it rained the wintry rain that drenched
    him through and through;
the crowds went home and left the streets without
    a soul to see,
    and Jesus crouched against a wall
    and cried for Calvary.

Geoffrey Studdert Kennedy

THE MAGNIFICAT

My soul doth magnify the Lord
    and my spirit rejoices in God my Saviour,
for he has been mindful
    of the humble state of his servant.

From now on all generations
    will call me blessed,
for the Mighty One has done great things for me –
    holy is his name.

His mercy extends to those who fear him,
    from generation to generation.
He has performed mighty deeds with his arm;
    he has scattered those who are proud
in their innermost thoughts.

He has brought down rulers from their thrones
    but has lifted up the humble.
He has filled the hungry with good things
    but has sent the rich away empty.

He has helped his servant Israel,
    remembering to be merciful
to Abraham and his descendants forever,
    even as he said to our fathers.

Luke 1:46-55

ACKNOWLEDGEMENTS

The publishers wish to express their gratitude to the following for permission to reproduce copyright material:

Hodder & Stoughton Ltd for scripture taken from the *Holy Bible, New International Version*. Copyright 1973, 1978, 1984 by International Bible Society. All rights reserved.

The Iona Community for *You want us to change* and *Faith and Works*, from 'The Iona Community Worship Book', © 1988 The Iona Community/Wild Goose Publications, 840 Govan Road, Glasgow, G51 3UT.

SPCK for *We turn to you O God* and *Glory be to you* from 'Women Included', © The St Hilda Community, published by SPCK 1991.

The Council of Churches for Britain and Ireland for *Not death throes but birth pangs*.

HarperCollins Publishers for *Creator, where shall I find you?* and *Our Father, it is your universe* from 'Heart of Prayer' by Anthony Gittins © 1985.

Christian Conference of Asia Youth, Hong Kong for *To live in community*.

Every effort has been made to trace the owners of copyright material and we hope that no copyright has been infringed. Pardon is sought and apology made if the contrary be the case, and a correction will be made in any reprint of this book.